HOW TO
Grow a Baby
JOURNAL

This journal belongs to:

· ·

INTRODUCTION

First, congratulations! Every pregnancy is so special and keeping a record of all the incredible changes that you go through both physically and emotionally over the next nine months – and as you start out on your journey as a new mum – is a lovely way to be able to look back and remember what happened when. It may not feel like it now (especially when you're in the throes of feeling sick or exhausted) but these 40-odd weeks – and those first few months with your newborn – will go past so quickly and you'll likely wonder 'did that really ever happen?'

You may be one of the lucky ones who 'glow' from the moment you find out you're pregnant and sail through the rest of pregnancy feeling the best you've ever felt… or you might find it tougher than you first imagined. Like any life-changing event, there are highs and lows and it's important to appreciate both as part of the amazing job your body is doing. That's why there are many opportunities in this journal to write down your feelings and thoughts, so you can capture, remember and reflect on them all. Try not to compare your pregnancy to others – remember everyone is different. Our bodies sense and feel things differently and that's normal and is what makes us unique. And the same goes for your unborn baby. Babies grow, develop and move in different ways. Each of my own pregnancies was as different as the personalities of my daughters today!

Treat this journal like a memory box to keep all those important 'firsts' in one place. Your first scan, the first time you felt your baby kick, the first babygro you bought. There are also lots of lovely opportunities to add photos of your growing bump and your new baby too. You'll be amazed when you look back and see the difference! There are week-by-week tips for getting through each trimester, empowering positive affirmations from YESMUM, easy recipes and a place for you and your partner to write your birth stories.

Sometimes pregnancy can feel like it's all about you, but there is another parent in the mix and their feelings and emotions are equally as important. Taking the time to talk together about what you're both going through will hopefully prompt you to really find out how each other is feeling about this huge and exciting change that is about to happen – and not just go round in circles choosing baby names (we've all been there!). Use some of the questions in this journal to help keep you connected during your pregnancy and once your baby is born.

After you've brought your baby home from the hospital – or settled in after a home birth – the adventure is just beginning! This journal continues through the first months after your baby is born – now known as the fourth trimester – and which can quite often feel like a blur. Recording what's going on in those early days, even in the midst of the chaos or when you're tired during a 3am feed, may feel mundane at the time, but they are such special days that will go past in a flash. There's also space to write down your baby's weight so you can chart his or her growth, the first time they smiled, rolled over and maybe even slept through the night!

But, most importantly perhaps, this journal is for you and your child to look back through together when they are older and to remember this special time you shared. You can open up conversations about how a baby really does grow and fit in mummy's tummy, how you finally picked the perfect name and all those tiny but hugely important milestones you both achieved together.

Use this page to fill in all the important people in your baby's life.

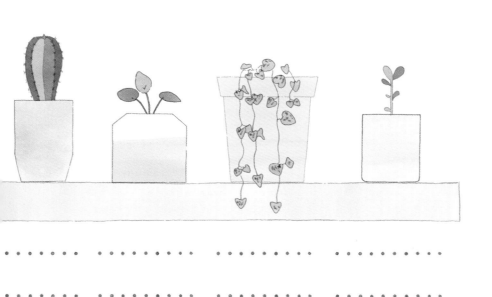

THE
FIRST
TRIMESTER

THE FIRST FEW WEEKS

The beginning of your pregnancy can feel like a funny old time. As soon as you find out you are pregnant, your mind is suddenly consumed with so many thoughts racing around: No more drinking. When should we tell anyone? I don't feel any different, am I even pregnant? Is it all going to be OK? No more Brie! It can almost feel overwhelming that something as tiny as a sunflower seed can consume so much of your emotional energy.

You may not have bought this journal (or kindly had it gifted to you!) until after your first scan at around week 12. That's usually the time most people relax a little bit into their pregnancy. So I suggest you go back and fill in this bit retrospectively, trying to remember all those feelings, fears and emotions you first felt in those very early stages. You'll soon forget how you felt as the pregnancy progresses so it's a really lovely way to look back and remember, and maybe even laugh or cry. Or both?!

Even though very little may be happening on the outside, there are a million things changing inside you as your baby starts to develop from a cluster of tiny cells into a baby with a beating heart. But until your 12-week scan, when most people will first get to see their baby, it can feel really strange – almost unbelievable – is there anything even growing in there?

But let's not get ahead of ourselves. The most important thing right now is that you slow down, take a breather and look after yourself. Your body is doing the most incredible job, and even though we women are designed to make, grow and birth babies, it can still feel like the biggest of all challenges.

As a midwife, I have cared for many women during their pregnancy and you wouldn't believe how many women ask me in those early days 'what am I supposed to be doing now?!' My usual response is 'not a huge amount'. Just try and relax and trust the process. Remember to rest and nurture your changing body, it's doing amazing things.

Increased hormones racing around your body can leave you weeping at the adverts on TV one minute and the next, losing your temper because your partner asked you what you want for dinner. Hormones can make you feel mental. But that's OK and completely normal. Try and talk to those around you. Even if your partner has no idea what to do, just explain why you're all over the place, whether that's feeling emotional, tired, hungry, sick, irritated or all of those things within 5 minutes of each other. Off-load to a good friend who's been there, she will understand more than anyone (OK, maybe apart from your mum) that it's OK to admit you feel scared or worried that every ache or pain means that something is wrong.

But don't let this stage of pregnancy go by as one big worry. You may not have much control over what's going on inside you, but try letting go of the things you can't control, and taking ownership of the things you can to nourish you and your baby.

* Get as much sleep (or at least rest) as your body is begging for. This may be the odd nap or going to bed at 7pm as soon as you're back from work – whatever it is your body needs, listen to it. It knows best!

* Eat what you can, and don't go overboard with trying to eat super healthily. Most women can't stomach a green kale smoothie at this stage of pregnancy so go for whatever you can keep down and don't worry if you live off toast and peanut butter or crisp sandwiches.

* Try some light meditation and breathing exercises, especially if you're feeling anxious. Anxiety is a bit of a mood killer so 'inhale peace, exhale tension'. Sometimes that's all it takes and the difference can be quite remarkable.

* Admire your body, thank it for being so clever at getting you pregnant and holding onto the bean-shaped blob that will become a baby. That is something quite special.

HOW YOU FOUND OUT YOU WERE PREGNANT

Discovering you are pregnant is both thrilling and terrifying. Whether you've been trying for a while or not, when those two pink lines show up loud and clear you can still feel like shouting 'oh my god' in disbelief! It can take some getting used to and that's totally normal.

Some women 'know' something's up as soon as they go off their favourite daily flat white coffee or when they suddenly need a 10-minute power nap during their tea break. (The overwhelming need to sleep is quite something!) For others, it might be the telltale sign that your period is late that prompts you to nip into Boots during your lunch break to buy a pregnancy test.

Don't worry if it all feels overwhelming right now. You have months to get your head around things and buy babygros. Nothing needs to happen right this instant, and it may not even feel real until you see your baby wriggling at your 12-week scan. Many women don't even feel that it's really happening until they feel their baby move at around 22 weeks. So try to relax and enjoy the building excitement of those early days. I mean, you're going to have a baby in approximately eight months! That is so bloody exciting! A brand-new, unique, never-made-before human that you will get to hang out with all the time. And you're going to be a someone's mama. That is seriously cool.

Where were you when you found out you were pregnant?

_____

What made you think you were pregnant?

_____

_____

How did you react and how did you feel?

_____

_____

_____

Who did you tell first?

_____

What did they say?

_____

_____

_____

FEELING SICK AND TIRED

Even though your tiny baby is only about the size of a kidney bean, the physical changes going on in your body can feel huge! Morning sickness is one of the most common symptoms during the first trimester, although this can manifest itself as all-day sickness and even vomiting. It can often be the hardest to deal with too because although it's all you can focus on, normal life must continue – and usually without anyone around you knowing you are pregnant yet.

During my pregnancy with the twins, I felt so sick most of the day but I was working full-time as a community midwife. I would see my women for their check-ups and then run back to my car and either heave over a drain or scoff ten fizzy sweets until I felt OK again. I managed to keep a professional manner for as long as the appointment and then all hell would break loose as soon as I was on my own, retching or puking in the street. I can no longer even look at that brand of sweets again, never mind eat one.

Sometimes the simplest of tasks, such as using public transport or cooking a meal, can be a challenge. It can feel like one long hangover! But it's all part of the fun of being pregnant, so try to take it in your stride. Knowing you're not alone can make it more bearable – I'm sure many women have whispered to a colleague in the staff kitchen 'did you feel like death when you were pregnant?' Maybe off-load to that one person you know has been there before, as you reach for another ginger biscuit. They will know exactly how you're feeling.

The good news is that by around 12 weeks these symptoms will usually have reduced and, in most cases, you will start to feel better. (Although some ladies will feel waves of nausea – or worse – throughout their whole pregnancy, and that's totally normal too.)

If you're feeling nauseous, eat little and often – try nibbles of biscuits or pieces of apple or banana. It doesn't matter hugely what you eat, as long as you put something into your body. And remember to keep hydrated: fresh lemon and lime in fizzy water and cold coconut water saved me in those early weeks. It's also a good idea to keep something by your bed, like oatcakes or breadsticks, for when you first wake up or if you wake in the night and feel sick.

The other very common sign that you're well and truly pregnant is feeling completely exhausted even after eight hours sleep. Needing a desk nap at 3pm is very normal. Your body is doing amazing things growing your baby and placenta, so listen to it and don't ever feel guilty about crawling off to bed at 8pm.

Hormones can play havoc with your mind even when you're not consciously thinking about pregnancy. Lots of women tell me their dreams are very surreal in the early weeks. One women kept dreaming she was giving birth to kittens! So if you think 'hang on, is this because I'm pregnant?' it probably is – your hormones are very powerful.

What are your main pregnancy 'symptoms'?

Are there any foods or drinks you've gone off?

What can't you eat enough of?! Any interesting cravings?
Favourite snacks?

If you have morning sickness, does anything help you feel
less queasy?

Any inappropriate stories of battling through those early weeks?

KEEPING IT
A SECRET OR NOT

Keeping something so exciting a secret is very difficult, and especially if your friends and family notice you refusing your regular glass of wine! It can feel hard deceiving those closest to you, especially when being pregnant is such a special time and you know that they only want to enjoy and share in your good news.

You may feel comfortable telling a few close friends early on, particularly those who have had babies themselves, as they may be able to sympathise and offer tips for combatting the nausea and exhaustion or be able to buy you the infamous preggo's fake 'G&T' (soda, lime and a slice of lemon)! Sometimes just being able to ask those trusted friends 'did you feel like this?' can be very comforting and reassuring.

But many women choose to wait until the 12-week scan before telling anyone. Sometimes waiting until you've got the 'your baby looks normal' result and a picture of your baby from the scan can be the reassuring information you need to then feel comfortable sharing the lovely news among those closest to you. And there's nothing quite like telling the future grandparents by popping a picture of the scan in their hand (cue sobs all round). Whatever you decide, it's up to you and your partner so make sure to discuss it together.

Who did you tell first, after your partner?

Best reactions?

Any funny stories about keeping it a secret?

Did anyone guess?

Did you or your partner give it away by accident?

THE 12-WEEK SCAN

How did you feel in the waiting room before being called in?

_____

_____

What was your initial feeling when you saw your baby on the screen?

_____

Did the baby look how you imagined?

_____

What tests (if any) did you have?

_____

Did your partner try to crack any jokes/say anything inappropriate?

_____

How did you feel immediately afterwards?

_____

_____

18

STICK
YOUR SCAN
PICTURE
HERE

THE
SECOND
TRIMESTER

YOU'VE MADE IT TO WEEK 12!

YOUR BABY IS ABOUT THE SIZE OF A LIME

It may not feel like a huge achievement (especially if you've spent the last few weeks with your head over the toilet and nibbling on ginger biscuits) BUT getting to this stage is a massive step. By now, you should have had your scan and will hopefully feel confident enough to start sharing the lovely news with friends and family. Most women find that once they reach 12 weeks, those horrible pregnancy symptoms start to lessen and they begin to feel much better. You may get your appetite back too and feel ready to eat foods with flavour again (without the risk of vomiting five minutes later) and hopefully you'll feel a little more energised! Having not been able to cook for the past few weeks and surviving purely on jacket potatoes and crisps it may be nice (if you like cooking that is) to rustle up your favourite meals again. Sitting down with your partner for an evening meal is a lovely way to connect and talk about the pregnancy and maybe even discuss possible baby names…

The second trimester is when many women start to feel that 'glow', although it's worth mentioning that some women never experience this and find the whole of their pregnancy a bit of a struggle. If you're lucky, you may notice that your skin is the best it's ever looked. Or, like some other women, maybe your skin resembles more that of a pubescent angry teenager.

If your skin is super-sensitive, have a look at your skincare regime and think about changing to products suited to sensitive skin. Your regular make-up brand, normally fine on your skin, may suddenly bring you out in spots too, so consider laying off it for a while, or changing brands. All those extra hormones racing around your body have a lot to answer for! Sometimes it takes a few more weeks for your body to adjust to these extra hormones so try and be patient.

You may also feel a little overwhelmed by all the things you think you should be doing now, but remember there is no rush and it's important to take each step at a time. At this stage, you really don't need to know what pram you are going to buy. The only really important thing to have done by now is to have accessed your maternity care and been booked in by your midwife.

On the good days, when you feel well and have lots of energy, try and focus on these positive moments and marvel about how brilliant your body is. Growing a human should never be taken for granted. Your body is amazing and so are you.

What are some moments you've loved so far about being pregnant?

_____

_____

_____

Are there any moments you've not enjoyed so much?

_____

_____

_____

Is there anything that's surprised you?

_____

_____

_____

Is there anything that has surprised your partner?

_____

_____

Is there anything you miss about not being pregnant?!

‐ ‐

‐ ‐

‐ ‐

What are you looking forward to in this next trimester?

‐ ‐

‐ ‐

‐ ‐

‐ ‐

‐ ‐

‐ ‐

‐ ‐

‐ ‐

‐ ‐

‐ ‐

WEEK 13

YOUR BABY MAY START TO SUCK HIS OR HER THUMB

Acknowledging the milestone of entering your second trimester should be celebrated! If you're feeling up to it, why not book a meal with your partner or a friend at your favourite restaurant? You may feel like you're coming out of your shell a bit now, especially if you've felt sick, tired and generally rubbish for the past few weeks. You – and those around you! – will enjoy seeing a bit of the 'old' you again. Throw on something that makes you feel a bit special – but if all you want to wear is black stretchy trousers, then add a bright lipstick or fun piece of jewellery. And it may be a good idea to book an early table so you can be in bed by 9pm!

What did you decide to do?

If you had a meal, did you avoid anything on the menu?
What did you eat?

Did you only talk about the pregnancy?

If you celebrated with your partner, how did it to feel to connect as a couple?

YOUR BABY IS ABOUT THE SIZE OF A LEMON

Although your maternity leave may feel like a long way off, it's so much better to get organised now and start doing your research, as it's the last thing you want to be doing when you're massively pregnant or with a newborn baby. In the UK, every pregnant employee is currently entitled to 26 weeks of ordinary maternity leave. You can then take an extra 26 weeks of additional maternity leave, giving you a year's leave in total. But you must give your employer the correct notice via a form called a Mat B1, which is given to you signed by your midwife or GP when you reach 21 weeks into your pregnancy. Make sure to ask for it if they don't give it to you. If you are self-employed or unemployed during your pregnancy you may be able to claim maternity allowance. This can be paid from 11 weeks before your baby is due for up to 39 weeks. Check out gov.co.uk for more information.

Don't forget that you're also entitled to free prescriptions and dental care up until your baby's first birthday. Speak to your midwife or GP who will get you the right forms to fill out so you can get your Mat B1 card.

How do you feel about going on maternity leave?

_____

_____

_____

If you work, how do you feel about time away from your job?

_____

_____

_____

What are you most looking forward to about maternity leave?

_____

_____

Anything you are not looking forward to?

_____

_____

_____

WEEK 15

YOUR BABY IS STARTING TO HEAR THINGS

As part of appreciating your changing body, you will definitely need to invest in some new underwear. Some women love their new shape! While for others it can take a bit of time to adjust. If you haven't already done so, make sure you go and get yourself properly measured for a new bra. I advise women to get measured at least twice: early on (as soon as their usual underwear starts to feel uncomfortable) and again at around 34–36 weeks. Don't be disheartened by the lack of choice in the shops – it's all about comfort at this stage. Take a close mate with you who has been there before for moral support. You can find some really pretty crop tops around too, which can be good to sleep in if you need a bit more support at night.

Where did you buy your first maternity bra?

--- ---

What is it like?

--- ---

Were you surprised by the size you were fitted with?

--- ---

--- ---

How did you feel when you put it on?

--- ---

--- ---

Any funny moments in the changing room?

--- ---

--- ---

--- ---

--- ---

One of the things I really regret with each of my own pregnancies is not taking more photos of my ever-changing bump. We've all seen those wonderful weekly or monthly bump shots shared online. They really make you realise how impressive your body is during those 40-odd weeks of pregnancy and how quickly it changes, often without you even really noticing. Try getting into the habit of taking a side-view photo every week or so in front of a full-length mirror. You may also want to be consistent and wear the same outfit or something fitted so you can really see how much your bump changes and grows. Imagine being able to look back with your partner or when your child is older and have 30 or 35 photos of your bump! It may feel like a bit of a chore now but it will be lovely to have as a keepsake.

How do you feel about your growing bump?

STICK YOUR
BUMP PHOTO
HERE

YOUR BABY IS THE SIZE OF AN AVOCADO

Although some women choose to wait until they've had their 20-week scan before they tell people they are pregnant, many women will have shared the news with at least a few people by now. And as soon as you start to tell people, it can often seem as though the world and his dog has an opinion on pretty much everything to do with your pregnancy! Your colleague that you've never spoken more than three words to will start telling you in the lift about which antenatal classes he and his wife found the best when they had their baby. Your hairdresser will name every single pregnancy complication she experienced during her own pregnancies, including piles and swollen ankles. It can be quite tricky to know how to navigate this new-found attention and – often unsolicited – advice so try and smile sweetly and not let it get to you. Only you know your body best.

What was the best piece of advice someone gave you?

_____

_____

_____

And what was the worst?!

_____

_____

Do people treat you differently when they find out you're pregnant?

_____

_____

_____

How do you feel about the extra attention?

_____

_____

_____

BABY NAMES

TIPS ON COMPROMISING ON BABY NAMES:

- Never sound off a name to anyone(!). Opinions will divide even those closet to you.
- Teachers have the most opinions on names, as they will have taught every naughty Jack, Josh and Joseph.
- Try not to please the whole family. This is your baby and your decision.
- Pick your top three for each gender and then talk through why you both love them so much.
- Have a reserve list of names that you like but don't love.
- Give it time. Names grow on you and names you originally love you could go off by 40 weeks.
- Don't over think it; it makes it harder to decide. Leave it for a few weeks and come back to the list.
- And remember: just because you love someone, doesn't mean you'll agree on baby names!

GIRLS

BOYS

WEEK 17

YOUR BABY IS GROWING EYELASHES

Relax… Easier said than done, I know, but trying to relax in pregnancy can have a really positive impact on you and your baby. Some levels of stress are normal in our daily lives but research has shown that high levels of stress in pregnancy can affect your unborn baby. Try taking small but simple steps every day to keep calm and balanced. Some self-care tips include:

- Exercise – get moving, even if it's just a 10-minute walk.
- Get to bed early – grab a good magazine, maybe some snacks, avoid a screen, get into your comfiest PJs and rest.
- Listen to some calming music – create a playlist called 'me time'. It will be useful in early labour too.
- Try some light meditation – slowing down from the hectic lives we all lead and being more in the 'now' can be so beneficial to your state of mind and physical wellbeing.
- Repeat some positive affirmations – it's as easy and simple as taking a few minutes every morning (before looking at your phone or laptop) to read a YESMUM affirmation out loud such as 'Today I will slow down and try not to rush'. It's amazing what a difference it can make to your day.

Is anything specific about your pregnancy making you anxious?

_____

_____

_____

Who have you discussed this with?

_____

How are you dealing with any feelings of stress?

_____

_____

_____

What do you plan to do this week to help you relax?

_____

_____

_____

WEEK 18

YOUR BABY MAY START TO REACT TO
MUSIC AND OUTSIDE NOISES

The changes to your body at this time can feel huge, even if you don't yet have a big bump for all the world to see. Your usual clothes will probably be starting to feel a bit tight and if this isn't your first pregnancy, you may start to show sooner than last time. You may be desperate to buy some new maternity clothes, but you are likely to be still in that in-between stage where your normal clothes are too small but the maternity clothes you've tried on are so huge and floaty you can't imagine ever having to wear them.

Some days, you'll marvel at the amazing job your body is doing. And then on other days you'll just feel fat, and that can be hard to accept, especially as you might feel like you have no control over what is happening. But don't let it get you down. Remember that you're doing exactly what you're supposed to be doing to grow your baby. Learn to let go of these changes and accept them in all their beauty. Trust the process: your body is changing exactly the way it should. Comfort is key though, so when it comes to what to wear, opt for light, soft materials.

What are the biggest changes to your body so far?

Can you see a bump yet? Is it how you imagined?

How do you feel about your changing shape?

What's your favourite item of pregnancy clothing?

WEEK 19

YOUR BABY HAS STARTED TO GROW HAIR
ON HIS OR HER HEAD

Your 20-week scan is just around the corner now, and this will mark another major milestone in your pregnancy journey. You're almost halfway through! You may be feeling a bit anxious this week about the upcoming scan but try to relax as much as you can. One question friends and family will undoubtedly be asking you around this time is 'will you find out the sex of your baby?' Ah! It's such a tough decision, especially if you and your partner have opposite opinions on this subject. Some people choose to find out so they can prepare a sibling for the new arrival or they think it will make them feel more connected to their baby. Others feel that there are so few genuine surprises in life that they want to keep it a mystery! Whatever you decide, you both need to be 100 per cent sure of your decision because if you do decide to find out, once you're told, there's no going back!

Do either of you particularly want to find out/wait?

Why would you choose to find out?

Why would you choose to wait?

What did you decide?

THE 20-WEEK SCAN

YOUR BABY IS THE LENGTH OF A BANANA

How did you feel before you went in for the scan?

_____

_____

_____

Did you find out the sex of the baby?

_____

_____

What did you think when you saw the baby on the screen?

_____

_____

How did it differ from your 12-week scan?

Did you think you could see some features of the baby's face
that looked familiar?

What was the sonographer like?

How did your partner feel?

Did anything else funny or memorable happen during or after the scan?

How did you feel immediately afterwards?

STICK
YOUR SCAN
PICTURE
HERE

YOU ARE HALFWAY THERE!

And that is a fantastic achievement! Although it may feel a little daunting that there is going to be an actual human arriving in roughly 20 weeks, be proud of the fact that you've already grown your baby from a tiny poppy seed to a banana!

Growing a baby is pretty full-on, and it can often feel like you're doing all the hard work while your partner carries on as normal, without having to give up alcohol and soft cheeses, and without falling asleep at 8.30pm.

It's a nice idea to acknowledge this milestone with a treat to yourself *from yourself* for doing all this hard work.

SOME IDEAS INCLUDE:

- Have a manicure or pedicure – gorgeously painted nails are an instant pick-me-up (go for something bright!).

- Meet a really good friend for lunch – catching up over a delicious lunch is a perfect way to spend an afternoon.

- Go and buy some maternity clothes – it's time to dress up that bump and the choices out there are better than ever before.

- Have a massage from a qualified therapist or from your partner – you might find your back is already a bit achy at the end of a busy day and a massage is the perfect way to ease any discomfort.

- Get into the habit of having a bath every evening using essential oils – citrus oils, lavender, jasmine or eucalyptus are good choices. It's a great way to introduce oils that you can then use in labour to help you relax. (Check they are safe to use in pregnancy.)

- Look into finding a local pregnancy yoga or Pilates class – not only are the techniques taught perfect for preparing for labour, it's also a lovely gentle way to meet and make friends with other pregnant women in your area.

Remember that it's normal to feel a bit overwhelmed by pregnancy at times; after all, it's down to you to do all of the hard work. So try to make time just for you. Treating yourself is really important for your sanity and happiness!

Getting to know your bump is like a preview to getting to know your baby once he or she is born. Everyone's pregnancy bumps are different shapes and sizes so try not to compare yours to the woman sat next to you in yoga. And if you haven't already found out what you're having, no matter how many people try and convince you, there is no way to determine the sex of your baby by the way you're carrying!

How do you feel about your growing bump?

STICK YOUR
BUMP PHOTO
HERE

YOUR BABY IS PRACTISING HOW TO BREATHE

Feeling happy, scared, nervous and excited are all completely normal emotions to feel at this stage of pregnancy – after all you're now over halfway there and suddenly you might be feeling like this pregnancy is really happening! The thought of there being a baby at the end of this journey can often feel totally bizarre, almost unimaginable, but research shows that the earlier you connect with your bump in your pregnancy, the quicker you will bond with your baby when he or she is born. You may have started to feel the baby move at this stage, which can feel really special, so try chatting to your bump when you feel those wriggles: 'Hello baby, are you in there?' Get your partner involved too. Pregnancy can often feel quite abstract for the other parent so set aside some evenings this week for getting to know your bump together. Some people choose a nickname for their unborn baby, which can help you feel another level of connection with it, especially if you don't know the gender. Some classic names include prawn, squidge, peanut etc. Feel free to pick your own!

(Also, remember to ask your your midwife or GP for your Mat B1 form if you haven't received it yet.)

How are you feeling at the halfway point?

Do you have a nickname for your baby?

What do you do to connect with your bump?

How does your partner bond with your bump?

What do you like best about your bump?

YOU, YOU, YOU

It can often feel like once you become pregnant everything must change, and that can feel a bit weird. Up until now, you've been the boss of you. The restrictions you are experiencing can sometimes feel annoying and frustrating. The old you just wants to go out and enjoy a few drinks or even just to stay up past 10pm occasionally, but now you're having to think about somebody else, somebody that isn't even born yet, but who requires so much from you already.

Pregnancy is not only about the physical changes, it also gives you nine long months to start preparing emotionally for how it might feel when you become a mother. There's no getting around the fact that a newborn baby requires a lot from you and it can often take a while to adjust to your new life so it's good to start thinking about it now. Life is going to shift a few notches and you definitely won't be the first pregnant woman to feel like this as you're wandering around Mothercare not really knowing how you ended up there.

BUT it doesn't mean the old you has to be put aside and forgotten about! The old you is still in there and it's important you hold onto those aspects of your identity that are most important to you. OK, so you won't be able to get right back to living exactly the same life as you were pre-baby, but it's also not all over!

It's completely normal to question these emotions and feelings and it's completely normal to worry that you'll never be able to go out and see a friend ever again. I was convinced I'd never be able to talk to my friends about anything non-baby related, but over time I did and I now enjoy my children-free time just as much as I enjoy spending time being a mother.

The next chapter in your life is going to be exciting and, yes, you'll probably be tired and maybe a bit scared at first, but remember that underneath all of that you'll still be you, you'll just also be someone's mama and that's pretty special.

YOUR BABY IS STARTING TO GROW FINGERNAILS

This week spend some time thinking about all the ways that you will still be you, even when you become a mum. Having a baby doesn't mean you're going to suddenly become a completely different person! One way of helping the transition into motherhood is to try to make time for doing even just a few of the things you love to do. Maybe you won't be up for rock climbing or getting back on your skateboard immediately after the birth, but you can still go to your local café, meet up with friends (although maybe for a cup of tea rather than a cocktail!), listen to your favourite music and eat all your favourite foods. Often these simple steps can help you feel like you again.

What are you looking forward to most about being a mum?

What are you looking forward to doing when you're no longer pregnant?

Is there anything you feel like you'll miss out on doing once your baby is born?

What four things are you going to try to make time for once your baby is born?

1 ---

2 ---

3 ---

4 ---

YOUR BABY MAY START TO HAVE HICCUPS

Feeling your baby move is very exciting. Your baby will have its own individual habits and it can be difficult to recognise its movements at first. Lots of women find that once they stop, slow down and concentrate they can feel their baby move more, especially in the evenings. Another tip to encourage movement is to lie on the sofa or your bed (with some pillows under you so you're not too flat) and talk to your bump. You might find your baby reacts to music too, so play some of your favourite songs and encourage your partner to sing to your bump! You might not feel the baby move immediately but if you lie there long enough, you'll hopefully feel a few little flutters, nudges or even bigger movements like a kick! Some babies take a little longer to get going though so don't worry if you can't feel anything straightaway.

When did you first feel your baby move? What were you doing?

--- ---

What does it feel like? How does it make you feel?

--- ---

--- ---

Are there any songs/noises/TV theme tunes that it seems to react to?

--- ---

--- ---

Are there any foods that make your baby move around more after you've eaten them, such as spicy or sweet foods?

--- ---

--- ---

Is there anything your partner does that seems to make your baby respond?

--- ---

--- ---

ALMOND, MIXED SEEDS AND CHOCOLATE SQUARES

• • • • • • • • • • • • •

This easy no-bake treat is high in protein from the almonds and seeds. The chocolate – as well as satisfying those cravings – is also a source of iron. These make a great little energy boost for when you have a newborn baby too!

Makes 16
50g ground almonds
60g coconut oil, melted and cooled a little
170g smooth almond butter
1 tbsp maple syrup
4 tbsp mixed seeds, lightly crushed
100g dark chocolate, broken into pieces

Line a 15cm square dish with baking paper. (If you don't have a dish small enough, then you can make folded foil walls to the right size inside a larger dish.)

In a bowl, mix together the ground almonds, coconut oil, almond butter (reserving 2 tablespoons), maple syrup and the seeds. Pour into the lined dish and chill in the fridge.

Meanwhile, melt the chocolate either in a microwave or in a small heatproof bowl set over a pan of simmering water – don't let the bottom of the bowl touch the hot water or you could burn the chocolate. Mix well with the reserved almond butter then pour over the almond base.

Chill in the fridge until set – preferably overnight but for a minimum of 3 hours. Slice and store in an airtight container in the fridge for up to a week.

YOUR BABY IS AS LONG AS A CORN COB

By now, even the most unobservant colleague will have noticed that you're not just putting on a bit of weight specifically around the tummy area: you are, indeed, pregnant.

You've probably already handed in your signed Mat B1 form to the relevant person, but if not, don't panic, as this is the last week to do it. From now on, it will seem like everyone will start asking you when you're leaving to go on maternity leave.

Planning your exit from work can feel a bit daunting – it's not a two-week holiday to Spain, it's AN ACTUAL BABY!! But it will be even better than a holiday to Spain. OK, so you won't come back with a sun tan and a bottle of Rioja, but you will have a baby that you have created, grown and birthed. That beats any holiday.

When did you decide to share with your colleagues that you were pregnant? How did you tell them?

Did any of them guess already?

Was anyone surprised? What did they say?

How long have you planned to take off work?

When is your last day at work?

KEEPING ACTIVE

Keeping active is not only good for the body, it's also good for the mind as it releases happy hormones known as endorphins, which make you feel GREAT. No one is expecting you to take up spinning or body pump in pregnancy (and these are not usually advised at this stage anyway!) but anything from going for a long walk, having a swim or stretching out your pregnant body in yoga or Pilates will do the trick (just make sure you go to classes suitable for pregnancy). By the end of a busy day your hips and back can start to feel tight, sore and achy, and doing some simple stretches can really make a difference to tired joints. Or try out the home exercises on the opposite page that are safe to do when pregnant.

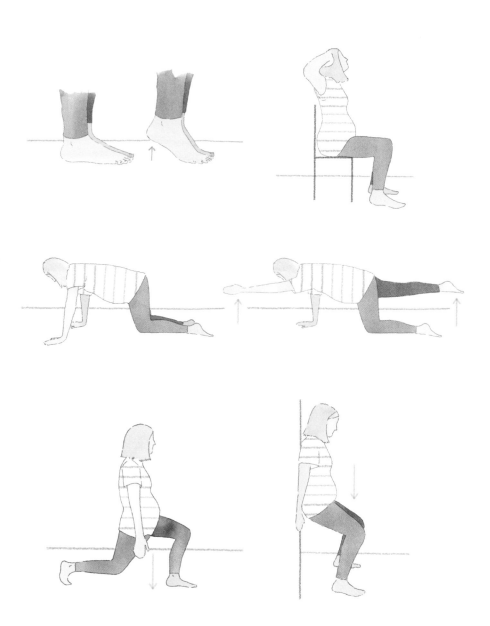

YOUR BABY IS DEVELOPING TASTE BUDS

Now your bump is starting to grow more rapidly, it's time to start thinking about caring for your ever-stretching skin. You may have already bought various lotions and oils to help prevent stretch marks and getting your partner involved is a lovely way to both feel your bump and even get some extra kicks from baby!

Research shows that preventative measures are the key to warding off stretch marks. Coconut oil, cocoa butter and creams especially designed for pregnancy are some of the best ways to prevent those red and pink marks. But don't just aim for your bump: hips, thighs and boobs get bigger too so slather it all over – you may feel like a slippery fish so go for a nice-smelling cream or oil!

Have you noticed any stretch marks yet? If so, where?

_____

Has your belly button started to changed shape? How?

_____

What is your favourite cream or oil?

_____

How do you feel about your growing bump and changing shape?

_____

_____

_____

_____

How does your partner feel about it?

_____

_____

_____

BUMP PHOTO 3 → WEEK 25

By now your bump is probably starting to reveal itself properly and you are likely to be getting more smiles and comments from people in the street. It seems everyone loves a pregnant person! Enjoy this time as it will go very quickly.

How has your bump changed from week 20?

_____

_____

_____

STICK YOUR
BUMP PHOTO
HERE

WEEK 26

YOUR BABY WEIGHS AS MUCH AS A CABBAGE

I know that making friends with other pregnant women can sometimes feel a bit fake. After all, all you really have in common is that you conceived at around the same time and now go to the same yoga or antenatal class! But creating a good network of other people who are going through the same thing as you can be incredibly supportive – for both you and your partner. And after you've had the baby, these are the people you can turn to if you're ever feeling overwhelmed, as they'll be facing exactly the same highs and lows. Meeting up for an emergency coffee or walk in the park can really turn your day around. They may even become such good friends that you go on holidays together, are asked to be their baby's godmother and go to many children's parties over the years. It's amazing how life-changing becoming a mother can be, and sharing it with others who are going through the same experience makes it all the more enjoyable.

What classes (if any) are you going to?

Have you met any new friends?

What are your first impressions?

How has making friends with other pregnant women helped you?

Has your partner made friends with any of the partners of your pregnant friends? How have they found it helpful?

WEEK 27

YOUR BABY CAN NOW RECOGNISE YOUR VOICE

As you head into the third trimester it is a good time to start gathering all the information you need to help you feel confident during these final stages and as you get ready for the birth. Next week you'll be seeing your midwife for your 28-weeks blood test, so this is also a good opportunity to ask some important questions to help you feel prepared. Ask whatever you feel you need to know, but some suggestions include:

- Is there a tour of the hospital birthing unit? Do you have to book? When is it recommended you go?
- What is the recommended way to travel to the hospital when in labour? Is parking available?
- If you're planning a trip, is it safe to fly at this stage? Do I need a letter from my midwife?
- Do I need to carry my hospital notes everywhere I go? Even when travelling in the UK?
- Are there any free breastfeeding classes provided by the hospital? Can partners come too?
- What books or websites would you recommend for preparing for birth? Do the hospital provide NHS birth preparation classes?

What other questions do you want to ask?
Write them here so you don't forget:

1 --

----

2 --

----

3 --

----

4 --

----

5 --

THE
THIRD
TRIMESTER

You're now into the third trimester, the final stretch before your baby will be born! Sounds scary but there is still lots of time to get organised, feel prepared and embrace welcoming your baby into your life. Now is also the time to start really thinking about yourself and listening to what your body needs. Get into the habit of going to bed early with a good book or your hypnobirthing soundtrack – being pregnant is the perfect excuse to get out of events you don't want to go to! Keep focusing on all the positives in these final few weeks. Early in the third trimester, you may still feel quite energised and lots of women say their skin and hair looks the best it ever has. Many women also find they don't need to wax or shave as much either – a definite plus in my book (also, it's pretty hard to shave your legs with a big bump in the way!).

BREATHE

Undoubtedly, you're beginning to feel much bigger now and are probably wondering how on earth you're going to look when you're full term, and you may even be starting to worry about the birth. Your body is amazing so TRUST it to know what to do: women are designed for this.

Get into the habit of breathing well, as this will really help you during labour. As your baby grows and your uterus expands, your lungs are being squashed, which can sometimes make it feel like you can't breathe as well as normal, especially when climbing up the stairs or up a hill. Placing your hand on the top of your bump and counting your breath in for four and out for six is a great little exercise for calming yourself down, relaxing and simply remembering how to breathe properly. Continue to exercise when you can too. This might be your weekly Pilates or yoga class, a home DVD or online video you've been following. Lots of pregnant women enjoy swimming at this stage in pregnancy as the water takes your weight and it can be incredibly soothing on tired aching muscles. Keeping fit will also help you during labour.

OFF-LOAD

Any worries you may have at this stage are completely normal and you won't be the first pregnant woman to think of them, however out there you may think they are! Chat things through with your partner. Remember those added hormones? They have a funny way of making things seem unmanageable at times, but talking to those closest to you or with someone who's been pregnant before can really help. Knowing you're not alone is reassuring – but always ask your midwife or GP if you are concerned.

REST

Start getting into the habit of having naps. Regardless of whether you actually feel tired or not, you'll be amazed at how quickly you can nod off on the sofa or in bed. And even if you can't actually sleep, try to rest your body. Leave your phone in another room, read a magazine or, even better, listen to some light mediation or hypnobirthing downloads. It is also a great way of teaching your body to nap when your baby naps (you'll need all the extra zzz then).

How do you feel heading into the final few weeks?

What are your biggest concerns right now?

What are you most excited about or looking forward to?

How do you feel compared to when you entered your
second trimester?

How does your partner feel?

ASK THE MIDWIFE

You may have a million questions racing around your head and chances are at some point you'll wonder 'is this normal?' Here are some of the most frequently asked questions and worries I discuss with women in their third trimester. It may feel hard right now, in this final slog but, I promise you, the end is in sight.

Does my bump look too big/too small?
This is unlikely unless your midwife has previously highlighted an issue requiring you to go for extra growth scans. We are all different heights and weights and so are our bumps.

How will I know when I'm in labour?
It usually starts with period-type pains, which then become contractions and don't go away. It sounds weird but most women just 'know'. You are more tuned into your body than you think.

I haven't written my birth plan yet, does that matter?
Not at all! You've got weeks until you need to be writing this.

I haven't bought a pram/cot/car seat/single item for the baby!
The magic of the internet is next day delivery! Good friends will rally round and lend you things too. You'll be amazed at how easily you can buy the essentials for a baby from most high-street shops and supermarkets.

I keep snacking on biscuits, is that really bad?

A packet of chocolate biscuits every day isn't the wisest of snacks but don't beat yourself up for having a few if you get the urge.

How will the baby fit though my pelvis?!

The body is brilliant at making this work. Your baby's head – the heaviest part – usually engages at around 38 weeks, which allows it to sit nicely in your pelvis. The head is also quite soft and the skull bones overlap to make it smaller when being pushed out.

Will my body ever look the same again?

Some women seem to snap back into shape and look like they never gave birth, but often these are images we see in the media of celebrities who have a personal trainer and a chef to help them along. Of course your body will change through being pregnant, but many women say they actually prefer their post-baby bodies, as they are so proud of what they have achieved.

What if I can't breastfeed?

How you feed your baby is your decision. But also know that there is lots of support out there if you do want to breastfeed but are finding it difficult.

I'm worried about how different my life will be.

Of course your life and priorities will change, but it usually always happens in a way that feels OK and remember that you will still be you! Be honest with your partner about how you're feeling – you'll probably find that they are feeling exactly the same as you.

YOUR BABY IS THE SIZE OF AN AUBERGINE

Low iron levels can make you feel breathless and tired, so your midwife will offer you a blood test to check your iron levels at this stage in your pregnancy. If you are hoping to have a home birth then it's particularly important that you have a good level of haemoglobin to cope with any blood loss during or after the birth. There are ways to give your body a boost in iron through your diet. These include:

- Eating red meat, fish, chicken, eggs, wholegrain bread, pulses, dark green leafy vegetables and fortified cereals.
- Keeping a bag of dried fruit (such as unsulphured apricots) in your bag or by your desk or bed for snacking on.
- Vitamin C helps your body absorb iron so drink a glass of fresh orange juice with your breakfast rather than tea or coffee, as they can reduce iron absorption.
- A smoothie is a great way to get a quick boost of vitamins and minerals. Add iron-rich ingredients such as kale (even better than spinach), as well chia seeds, avocado, banana and berries to cover all your bases! See page 167 for a recipe – just add kale!

Despite all your best efforts, you may find your iron levels still don't increase and your midwife will recommend you take iron tablets. Some women find these make them constipated though, so keep up your fluids and you might need to take a gentle laxative such as lactulose.

What are you eating to help keep your irons levels up?

_____

_____

What are you eating more of generally?

_____

_____

Have you developed a taste for foods you don't normally eat or like?
Or have you gone off any of your favourite foods?

_____

_____

_____

How has your appetite changed? Do you find yourself reaching for
the snacks? What are your go-to snacks?

_____

_____

_____

YOU AND
YOUR PARTNER

Unsurprisingly, your relationship with your partner will be put to the test at times while you're pregnant. Pregnancy can be difficult for both of you as you navigate all the changes going on both physically and emotionally, and as you think and plan ahead for your new life with your expanding family. Even if your baby was months (or even years) in the planning, it will all be starting to feel very real right about now. All those hormones racing around your body can also mean that your normally calm and sunny demeanour can flip to inconsolable weeping in all of a minute in the middle of the baby section of your local department store. Don't worry, the shop assistants will have seen it all before.

Try to remember that you're in this together, even if at times it feels like you're doing all the hard work. Make time to spend with each other, even if it's just watching your favourite TV show while your partner rubs your feet or feeds you ice cream. Some couples use this opportunity to go on a babymoon – perhaps a night away in a hotel or at a spa where you can just focus on the two of you (check with your doctor or midwife if you are planning on going anywhere further afield).

Remember to check in regularly with your partner to find out how they are feeling. They may not be big on talking about their feelings but try to encourage them to share what they're thinking. Although they may not be experiencing the obvious changes you are, it's still a big life event for them as well, so make sure to talk about anything you're both worried about and what you're both looking forward to. You're going to be parents soon! That's a pretty exciting adventure to be going on together.

SOME SPECIAL THINGS THAT YOUR PARTNER CAN LOOK FORWARD TO YOU DOING IN THE COMING WEEKS

* Crying for no apparent reason at random (and not always appropriate) moments.

* Making 'ugh' noises when trying to roll over in bed/pull up your maternity jeans/tying up your shoe laces.

* The uncontrollable farting, for which there's often very little or no warning.

* The middle-of-the-night panic 'HAVE WE BOUGHT ENOUGH MUSLINS/BABY GROWS/NAPPIES?!'

* The nesting: suddenly you have the most overwhelming urge to clean out the loft/shed/cupboard under the stairs despite being almost eight months pregnant.

* The wonderful moment when your baby gives an almighty kick just as your partner has their hand on your bump.

YOUR BABY CAN NOW OPEN HIS OR HER EYES

As the weeks go by, it can sometimes feel like everything is all about the baby. This week, aim to spend some proper time with your partner, checking in with each other to see how you are both feeling – and also just enjoying each other's company. Get out of the house and go and do something you used to enjoy doing pre-pregnancy, and try not to talk about the baby all of the time! Remember that you were a couple before you were pregnant and it's important for your relationship that not everything revolves around your bump… even though that can probably feel hard to imagine at the moment as it's the first thing either of you see in the morning!

What did you do this week with your partner to spend quality time together?

What kind of parents do you think you'll be?

What are you most looking forward to about being parents?

And what are you not looking forward to?

How do you think the baby will change your lives?

What can you do to ensure you still spend time together?

GETTING READY
FOR THE BIRTH

It's OK to feel a bit scared at this stage. Your bump is getting bigger, your back and pelvis are starting to ache at the end of the day and people might be asking you if you've decorated the nursery! But PAUSE, breathe and remember that this is the time to start thinking about the birth and not what colour pram you're going to buy or if your partner knows how to fit the car seat. None of those things really matter yet. Babies need very little when they're born despite what everyone else might be telling you!

It's really important that you know all about your options when it comes to birth. You'll be asked by your midwife to write your birth plan or preferences in the next five or six weeks so start to find out all the information you need to know.

Stay relaxed and remember that birth is always a bit unpredictable and does not follow a certain path that you may have seen set out in the books you've read or that is taught in your antenatal classes. Also remember that it is *your* birth so don't feel pressured to ask for something just because you've heard that your friend or a person in your yoga group did it.

Maybe you're hoping to have a home birth, use a birth centre or, on the advice of your midwife or doctor, give birth on the labour ward at the hospital? Lots of birth centres and hospitals arrange tours of the units, so ask your midwife if that would be possible. You maybe feel differently about where you want to give birth once you've viewed the space.

There are lots of resources out there to help and support you during this time. I really recommend finding a local hypnobirthing class and learning about useful breathing techniques for labour if you haven't already done so. It is so important in preparing for birth to learn how to breathe your way through it, and now is the time to start practising. Get your birth partner involved too, as they are the ones who will be able to bring you back into the space when you may be feeling out of control, scared or anxious. A simple breathing technique you can try at home is 'up-breathing': relax your shoulders and close your eyes, inhale through your nose to a count of four and then let the air out through your nose to a count of six. The longer exhale will work to quieten your mind and shut out distractions. This simple breathing exercise can be used at any stage in your pregnancy and is perfect for those moments when things can feel a bit much. It's also ideal for early labour.

You may also want to get a birthing ball to have at home to help get your baby into a good position. Try sitting on the ball in the evenings when watching TV, rather than slumping back on your sofa. Not only will it encourage your baby to move into the optimum position in your pelvis, it will also help with any aches in your lower back and hips.

Whenever you need a bit of a boost, read some positive affirmations out loud. Self-belief and confidence are great for dealing with those tricky moments all women feel at various points during their pregnancy. And repeating them now will mean they'll come into your mind when you're in labour without you even trying. Try placing cards

with encouraging and empowering phrases on them around your home – by your mirror, in the bathroom or on the fridge, or even on your computer at work. There are some throughout this book, or have a go at writing your own (see page 115).

The most important thing to remember is that birth is exciting and amazing and you will get to meet your baby at the end of it! Talk to your bump, connect with the baby you are growing inside you and tell it that everything will be OK. This is the time to thank your body for doing such a remarkable thing.

YOU CAN DO THIS.

Everything is
going to be okay.

I put all fear aside as I prepare for the birth of my baby.

YOUR BABY'S DIGESTIVE SYSTEM IS NOW DEVELOPED

Ah, sleep, that long-lost friend! At this stage of pregnancy getting a full night's sleep can start to feel like a thing of the past. You may be experiencing pregnancy insomnia – for no apparent reason, finding yourself wide awake at 2am, 3am or 4am. Lots of midwives believe this is the body's way of preparing for the broken sleep you go through with a young baby, but that's not a very helpful thing to hear right now while you're staring at the ceiling listening to your partner snore next to you. Your baby has also probably developed the delightful new skill of using your bladder as a mini-trampoline, which can result in you needing a pee every 30 minutes. Here are some tips for a better night's sleep:

* Get into bed earlier (no screens) and read something easy. Listen to a hypnobirthing or light meditation download – you'll be amazed at how instantly calming it is.
* Avoid caffeine – including chocolate – later in the day. And reduce your liquid consumption in the evening.
* Essential oils such as lavender, chamomile or orange are ideal for relaxing. Put a few drops on a cloth near your pillow and enjoy the scent.
* Everything can wait until tomorrow, so shut off your mind/ computer, ignore the chores and go to bed.
* Even if you're not asleep, your body is still resting so try not to worry about how much actual sleep you're getting.

How has your sleep changed in this trimester?

Do you have any favourite positions to sleep in?

What has helped you get more sleep?

What kind of dreams have you been having?

BUMP PHOTO 4 — WEEK 30

You may be surprised by how suddenly your bump is growing now. There's no denying it: you're most definitely pregnant! So, take a side-view photo in the mirror, or ask your partner to take it, and have it as a keepsake.

How are you feeling about your growing bump?

Can you see or feel any changes since your last bump photo?

STICK YOUR
BUMP PHOTO
HERE

WEEK 31

YOUR BABY CAN TASTE THE THINGS
YOU EAT VIA THE AMNIOTIC FLUID

Being pregnant is such a special time and those closest to you often want to share and celebrate your pregnancy with you. Why not gather a few special people together around this time? It doesn't have to be a huge occasion but it is a lovely way to connect with your girlfriends and/or family in the lead up to the birth. It can be a simple picnic in the park, a lunch or just tea and cake at home with your best friend. People want to spoil you when you're pregnant – and quite rightly too! If they do ask you for some suggestions for presents, here are some ideas:

- Some super-soft PJs or a new dressing gown.

- A gorgeous smelling candle.

- A voucher for a treatment, such as a pregnancy massage.

- Some home-cooked meals to pop in the freezer.

What did you do to celebrate your pregnancy?

_____

_____

How did it make you feel?

_____

_____

How did the attention make you feel?

_____

_____

Who organised it?

_____

Who was there?

_____

What gifts did you get?

_____

WEEK 32

YOUR BABY IS AS LONG AS A STALK OF KALE

Feeling your baby move inside you is something very special.
You may already know the pattern of your baby's movements and,
as you will have explored back in week 23, it's also a lovely way for
your partner to feel connected when touching your bump and feeling
a great big kick! You'll find you'll miss those movements after your
baby is born. As midwives, we remind women that these movements
are the most important way of you knowing that your baby is well.
They will gradually increase up to this stage, when they will then stay
the same until the birth. Every baby and pregnancy is different: my
first baby was a night-time kicker whereas my second moved mostly in
the mornings. As for the twins, they moved all day and all night long!
Keeping a note of how and when your baby moves or when he or
she is more or less active is a fun reminder to look back on, especially
for future pregnancies. It is also useful to keep a track of movements
during these final weeks so you can be aware if anything changes
and let your midwife know.

When is your baby the most active? And when is it quieter?

How has your baby's movements changed over your pregnancy?

How does your partner feel when the baby moves? And, if
you have another child, what did they think when they felt their
sibling kicking?

Does your baby respond to any particular voices or sounds?

YOUR BABY IS THE SIZE OF A PINEAPPLE

This week, despite having an achy bad back, insomnia and heart burn, I want you to focus on all the plus points of being pregnant because there are actually more than you might think!

- No more holding in your tummy! For once, wearing tight-fitting clothes and showing off your bump should be celebrated!

- You'll always get offered a seat on the bus or Tube.

- You can pretty much get away with saying 'the baby needs it' when tucking into a slice of cake.

- Letting off gas (from both ends) will always be excused.

- Having an afternoon nap on the sofa is definitely not lazy.

- And you can say 'I'm tired' as many times a day as you like.

- You can always use the toilet before anyone else in the queue.

- It's finally an excuse to go to the baby section at your local department store and coo over the tiny white babygros.

- You can blame all the tears on hormones. Animal rescue programme on TV? Long-lost families reunited after 50 years? Let it all out...

- Pregnancy leggings can be worn out of the house all the time.

- Massive cotton knickers are the only way to remain comfy and your partner can't bat an eyelid.

- You will always be made to feel special – what your body is doing is incredible.

List five of your favourite things about being pregnant:

1 _____

2 _____

3 _____

4 _____

5 _____

WEEK 34

YOUR BABY'S BRAIN HAS FULLY DEVELOPED

Breastfeeding is a wonderful and natural way to nourish your baby after she or he is born. You have everything you need to breastfeed your baby, but it is still a skill that you will need to learn, and education and empowerment are key to getting it right. Both you and your baby need to work together as there may be quite a few bumps along the road – with some easier than others to get over. But that's OK, there is plenty of help and support out there if you're struggling. Arming yourself with as much information as possible now can really benefit you both in the long run, so here are some suggestions:

- Watch some breastfeeding tutorial videos online such as: www.kellymom.com or www.laleche.org.uk.
- Go to a breastfeeding workshop. Most NHS hospitals run free classes.
- Understand what normal newborn feeding behaviour looks like. Not all babies eat exactly every three hours – they're babies not robots after all. Cluster feeding, for example, is very normal, especially during growth spurts.
- Find out what postnatal breastfeeding support is available in your local area. Ask your midwife or GP.
- Talk to friends who have been through it, and find out how they coped when things were difficult.

No one is expecting you or your baby to get it right straightaway. So give yourself time and know that it may take weeks in the beginning. Surround yourself with people who will support, encourage and look after you.

Here are some ideas to help you feel prepared – tick these off when you've done them!

○ Watch some tutorials online with your partner.
○ Find out about your local breastfeeding classes.
○ Find out what support is available to you for after the baby is born.
○ Discuss how your partner can help you.
○ Talk to someone who has breastfed before.

How are you feeling about breastfeeding?

YOUR BABY STARTS TO PRACTISE SUCKING MOVEMENTS

With only five or so weeks to go until you get to meet your baby (eek!) now is the time to start buying those essentials bits and pieces. Remember, you don't need to have everything brand new; second-hand can be just as good and saves on the pennies. If you're going shopping though, maybe ask your mum or a close relative or friend to go with you? Choosing that special first outfit that your baby will wear or come home from hospital in is a lovely thing to share with someone close to you. Babies don't really need much though — just lots of love and cuddles! — so there's no need to buy loads. You may even want to think about making something for the baby, such as knitting a blanket if your skills are up to it, or even a tiny hat. If you're not the crafty type, perhaps ask a family member if they'd like to — a personalised item is far nicer than shop bought and can be kept and passed on.

What did you first buy for the baby? How did it make you feel?

- -

- -

Have you been given anything from friends or family?

- -

Make a list of things you really need before the baby is born.
Some suggested essentials include:

- 5–10 cotton sleep suits and 5–10 cotton vests.
- 2 light-weight baby hats for immediately after the baby is born.
- Nappies (look out for offers in supermarkets – you'll never have enough nappies).
- Cotton cellular blankets and some swaddling muslins.
- Nappy cream, cotton wool pads, wipes.

BUMP PHOTO 5 WEEK 35

Hopefully you've been keeping a record of your bump throughout this pregnancy and can really see how it has expanded from the beginning to now! It's quite remarkable to see what changes we go through as women during pregnancy and how brilliant the body is at adapting to this new life growing inside us.

What do you like when you look at your bump in the mirror?

_____

Has your body changed in a way you weren't expecting?

_____

What has surprised you the most?

_____

What will you miss about your pregnant body?

_____

STICK YOUR
BUMP PHOTO
HERE

WRITING YOUR BIRTH PREFERENCES

Writing your birth preferences can feel like a surreal moment. You probably can still hardly imagine yourself giving birth, let alone an actual baby being born. But it's a really important way to start thinking about what you would 'prefer' to happen during labour.

Try and be open minded and flexible with your preferences. The best way of ensuring things go to plan is by acknowledging that they may not always go to plan, and that's OK, as birth can be unpredictable. For example, if option A or B hasn't worked then be prepared to go for option C. Allowing for these changes and having a few alternative scenarios in mind is important, as it will help you feel more positive about what does actually happen. You're having a baby, an actual human, and that is bloody amazing however he or she ends up coming out into the world.

Labour is hard work (hence the name), and you want your partner to be your voice during labour so you can channel your energy into working with your body and getting through the contractions, so make sure they are aware of your preferences. It's also a good idea to have a copy of your preferences handy for the midwife. Explore with your partner what both your priorities are and address any worries and fears. Fear is not your friend in labour, so use knowledge to feel empowered and in control: YOU CAN DO THIS!

Try not to allow other people's birth stories to feed any negativity into your own thoughts. This is your birth and everyone is unique. I have seen hundreds of births and each one is as special and as different as the next. And I always get the same fuzzy feeling when the baby is born, no matter what sort of birth it is.

And remember to never feel guilty about the choices you make on the day because they will always be the right choices at the time.

Writing your birth preferences with your partner is also a great way to discuss some key questions and think about the ways that they can help during labour. I've seen birth partners be great at giving their partners a back massage or reminding the midwife to dim the lighting in the room. Questions to consider include:

- Where would you like to have your baby – at home, at the birth centre or in hospital?
- Who is your birth partner or partners?
- What pain relief would you like to use?
- And what pain relief would you prefer not to use?
- Would you like your birth partner present for every examination?
- Would you like to use a ball, mats, beanbags or a birthing stool?
- Would you like to use a birthing pool?
- Would you like any photos or videos taken?
- Does your partner want to cut the cord?
- Would you like skin-to-skin with your baby immediately afterwards?
- How are you planning on feeding your baby straightaway?

WEEK 36

YOUR BABY IS ABOUT THE SIZE OF A ROMAINE LETTUCE

Packing your hospital bag is a very exciting moment, and one that all women build up to during their pregnancy. It can be a bit like packing for a holiday – but one where you don't know what the journey will be like or how long it is going to take to get there BUT where the destination is brilliant!

A good tip is to lay out all the essentials on your bed and then get your partner to pack the bag for you. That way they'll know exactly where everything is and it won't take them ages to find your lip balm or a hair band when you really need it. Below are a few pointers, but add whatever items you think you'll need (within reason!) to help you to feel as relaxed and comfortable as possible.

Here are my suggested essentials – tick them off when you've packed them, and write any other items you plan to take with you underneath.

- ○ Loose-fitting cotton nightie (a button-down one is handy for breastfeeding). Maybe consider packing a second nightie too, in case you have to stay in.
- ○ Big black cotton pants.
- ○ Comfy socks.
- ○ Maternity pads (you can never have enough of these).
- ○ A feeding bra.
- ○ Your washbag with all your essentials e.g. lip balm, hair band, hair brush and face wipes.
- ○ Essential oils e.g. lavender and clary sage.
- ○ A flannel, either for soaking in water to cool you down or dotting with essential oils.
- ○ A pillow.
- ○ Hot water bottle.
- ○ TENS machine.
- ○ Your hypnobirthing playlist and headphones.
- ○ Light snacks to keep you going, such as trail mix.
- ○ A change of clothes for when you leave hospital.

AT THE END OF THIS WEEK
YOUR BABY WILL BE FULL TERM

Affirmations are such a simple but effective way to shift your mindset to a place of positivity. Reading one out loud every day can give you that tiny fist pump you need, as if to say 'you can do this!' I really recommend repeating a few affirmations to yourself that resonate with you to help you start to feel confident as the birth approaches. The more you repeat them, the more you will start to see a real change in how you feel – which will carry you through birth and beyond.

Use some of the YESMUM cards included in this journal or have a go at writing your own, adapting them to your individual needs and concerns. Whatever your affirmation is, be sure to draw on the positive feeling it gives you and use it throughout your day. Try writing some down here and see how they make you feel – your affirmations should make you feel empowered, confident and in control.

MY AFFIRMATIONS

LISTEN TO YOUR BODY

Get ready to disconnect from the outside world and tune into your body and baby. I know this is easier said than done when the natural reaction is to fill your days with lunches and trips to Ikea. But use these final weeks to really slow right down. There is very little you *should* be doing now apart from resting and eating well.

The reality is that very soon you're going to go into labour and then you need to recover from birth and care for a baby. Think of these final weeks as your marathon preparation: nourish and nurture your body as it's about to do something incredible. Some gentle exercise is important for keeping your body engaged and active but don't exhaust yourself. Light yoga or a slow swim is ideal, plus you can practise your breathing. Getting things ready at home might seem essential but remember that getting *yourself* ready is so much more important.

NESTING OR RESTING?

Now would be the time to ask those around you to help you with any jobs that might need doing, such as putting together a cot, hanging up shelves or even tidying up the garden. Hopefully by now there are a few delicious meals in your freezer ready to be eaten during those first few weeks with your newborn but, if not, maybe ask your mum or a close friend to bring round some home-made meals to stash away for later.

IDEAS TO HELP YOU RELAX

- Listen to your hypnobirthing music and practise your breathing. This will also help keep you calm and focussed during labour.
- Ask your partner to massage you – every evening if possible!
- Have long relaxing baths.
- Eat a slice of cake!
- Talk to your baby, sing to your baby, tell it you're ready to meet him or her.
- Do some gentle exercise – swimming is ideal at this stage, as the water will help you feel lighter.
- Practise some light yoga or Pilates in a pregnancy class, or if you're really tired you could do it in the comfort of your own home.

It's important to remember to listen to your body. If some days you have bursts of energy, use that and focus it on doing an activity, but if you're so tired you can hardly face getting dressed then set aside that day to do nothing. Friends and family will understand if you have to cancel plans, so stay in bed, watch a million box sets and never feel guilty for this. You're amazing and remember what an incredible job your body has done so far. You're almost there.

CHICKEN AND SWEET POTATO TAGINE

• • • • • • • • • • • • •

Go easy on the spice if you plan on breastfeeding. This makes enough for four people so maybe portion it into halves before you freeze it. It is a good source of protein, iron, fibre, potassium, magnesium and zinc. You can leave out the chicken if you don't eat meat.

1 tbsp olive oil
2 onions, sliced into half moons
1 tsp rose harissa
3 skinless chicken breasts,
  chopped, or 8 skinless
  chicken thighs
½ tsp turmeric
½ tsp ground cinnamon
1 tsp dried mint
5cm piece of ginger, peeled
  and grated

zest and juice of 1 lemon
1 x 400g tin chickpeas,
  rinsed and drained
2 small sweet potatoes (375g),
  peeled and cubed
120g dried unsulphured
  apricots, halved
500ml water
salt and pepper
a small bunch of fresh
  coriander, to serve

Preheat the oven to 160°C(fan)/180°C/gas mark 4.

In an ovenproof pan (with a lid), heat the oil over a medium heat and fry the onions for 10 minutes or until softened. Stir in the harissa, cook for 30 seconds, then stir in the chicken pieces or thighs. Cook for about 5 minutes until slightly browned on all sides.

Stir in the turmeric, cinnamon, mint, ginger and half the lemon zest and cook for a few seconds. Add the chickpeas, sweet potato, apricots and water and season with salt and pepper. Cover and cook in the oven for 50 minutes, giving it a quick stir halfway through.

Remove from the oven, stir through the remaining lemon zest and the juice and the chopped coriander. Cool then freeze. Defrost fully before reheating thoroughly and serving with couscous or bulgur wheat.

WEEK 38

YOUR BABY CAN NOW GRIP WITH HIS OR HER HANDS

Creating a playlist is a lovely exercise for you and your partner to do together. Spend some time collecting all your favourite tunes ready for your labour. You may not think it now, but having music that makes you feel happy, focussed or active can be really beneficial for getting through each stage of labour.

Music has the ability to engage your emotions, so mix it up a bit. Try adding songs that have sentimental value to you both – your wedding music perhaps? Or upbeat music when you want to feel energised, and more chilled-out tunes for those early stages of labour when you're resting at home. To listen to the music, I've seen some women use mini portable speakers which attach to their phones or you can just use a pair of headphones.

Jot down your favourite pieces of music on the opposite page. Maybe include any songs that seem to make your baby move more, or are there any songs you'd love your baby to be born to?

MY PLAYLIST

WEEK 39

YOUR BABY IS THE SIZE OF A MINI WATERMELON

This week can feel a bit tough. With the 40-week mark just around the corner, your mind is probably all-consumed with your labour. You may be thinking any twinge is a sign that something is happening and you'll be checking your knickers every time you go to the toilet wondering 'is that my show?' I felt like everything was going to fall out down there by this stage and by the time evening came I was so achy and bloated I couldn't wait to have a bath and go to bed. You may also notice your rings don't fit on your fingers and your usual trainers are too tight as your hands and feet start to look at bit puffy. Some water retention is very normal, and I promise you your fingers won't resemble sausages for ever. Sometimes swelling can be a sign of pre-eclampsia though so do get it checked out by your midwife if you are concerned.

PLAN SOME ACTIVITIES TO TAKE YOUR MIND OFF THINGS, SUCH AS:

- Treat yourself to a pregnancy massage. It is just the best feeling, plus you might even fall asleep – double bonus!
- Book an afternoon tea with your best mates, eat delicious cakes and giggle about everything and anything.
- Get a manicure and pedicure – you will be thankful when you look down at your beautifully painted toes when you are in labour.
- Admire that bump in the mirror, take a selfie and marvel at your incredible body – look how brilliant you are!

You're almost at 40 weeks – how are you feeling?

How does your bump look now? Do you have any stretch marks?

How does the baby feel in your pelvis?

What have you done this week to take your mind off your due date?

Forty whole weeks, what an incredible achievement that is. You've done such an brilliant job so far, so try to remember this if you ever start to feel a bit anxious or if you find yourself wondering how on earth you got here!

You also may be thinking 'oh god, there's no going back now!' and suddenly the idea of pushing a baby out of your vagina doesn't seem like such a good idea. You may doubt everything – the choice of name, the colour you painted the nursery, your labour playlist, the snack bag BUT please know that it is totally normal to feel like this.

You may even start to resent your partner a little bit. I mean, after all, they get to swan about without a huge bump and the added weight and carry on as if nothing much has changed.

Feeling grumpy or angry or teary is completely normal too – and your partner will understand. Maybe ask them to give you a massage, or run you a relaxing bath or make you a nice dinner. And if you need to rant and vent sometimes, then let it all out! You're pregnant and probably a bit fed up by now and are longing to meet your baby.

All of this is *totally* normal and you won't be the first (or last) pregnant woman to behave in this way. Hormones can make you feel crazy at times, so just go with it, and know that this won't last for ever – you really are so, so close now. As hard as it may be at times, try to enjoy these last precious days of being pregnant – it really is such a fleeting time.

Don't focus too much on the due date. As you may have heard, only 5 per cent of babies are born on their due date – you're not a bag of popcorn ready to pop at 40 weeks! Treat it as an *estimated* due date – you may have another eight or nine days to go so try to find ways to relax and take your mind off it – easier said than done, I know!

Remember that your body knows what to do, so trust the process. Your baby actually releases a hormone to kick-start your body to go into labour – how clever is that?!

Make some plans that will help take your mind off your due date and give you something to look forward to, and if you have to cancel them because you're in labour then that's great!

Any time you feel stressed, focus on the hypnobirthing or relaxation techniques you've been practising. This may be when your phone pings for the tenth time that day from another well-meaning friend or relative asking if there's any news. Or when you're asking yourself 'how will I cope in labour?' Try turning your phone off, getting out of the house and going for a walk; just the change of scenery can clear your head of worries and thoughts.

Consider telling friends and family that you will let them know if anything changes or if you go into labour so they don't all contact you every day for an update. Keeping on top of your replies can sometimes feel like an added pressure, however good the intentions are of those around you. Conversely, you may feel like asking a close relative or friend to drop in on you every couple of days to see how you're getting on. Whatever you need to do is completely up to you and you'll be pleasantly surprised how people are more than happy to oblige and help out.

This is a very special time in pregnancy, so spend some quality time with your partner to help you both connect before the baby is born. A meal out (maybe at your local Indian to double up as a traditional way to bring on labour!), a visit to a beautiful park or a walk in the countryside are lovely ways to just be together. You may not want to talk about the baby (for a change) and instead chat about everything *but* the baby, the hospital bag and whether or not you think you've had a show. Try and enjoy these last few moments together as a couple.

HOW ARE YOU FEELING?

How have you felt this week, physically and emotionally?

_____

_____

_____

How does your bump look?

_____

_____

Any signs of labour?

_____

_____

How are you feeling about the birth? Excited, scared, ready?!

What have you done to stay relaxed?

How is your partner feeling?

How is your partner supporting you?

How have you stayed active?

WEEK 40 TICK LIST

YOUR BABY IS THE SIZE OF A SMALL PUMPKIN

You've arrived! This week spend as much time as you can relaxing and getting prepared for the birth. But sometimes sitting around the house can make you feel more anxious. Maybe invite a close friend or a relative over to take your mind off things for a while. Try and see someone or leave the house even if it's just to the corner shop to buy a pint of milk – the change of scenery can really help take your mind off staring at the empty Moses basket.

WHAT TO DO

○ Check your hospital bag is packed and ready.
○ Make sure you've seen your midwife for your 40-week appointment.
○ Check when to call the midwife/labour ward for when you think you're in labour.
○ Have you got enough frozen meals stashed in the freezer?
○ Do an online food shop to come for next week.
○ Plan how you're getting to the hospital – in your own car or a taxi? (Fit the car seat if necessary.)
○ Know the route to the hospital and the parking options.
○ Arrange child care/someone to feed the cat/dog/rabbit.
○ Practise your hypnobirthing relaxation techniques.
○ Tell yourself that 'baby comes when baby is ready' every single day you go past your estimated due date.

WHAT TO LET GO OF:

- DIY – put the hammer down and get someone else to hang those pictures.
- Unanswered emails? Put your out-of-office on.
- Worried you haven't got enough nappies/muslins/vests? You can always buy more online once the baby is born.
- Haven't had a wax? Don't bother – it's too painful and the midwives really won't care AT ALL.
- Haven't read the 'guide to being the perfect mother'? Forget it, it's a myth anyway.
- The tenth unanswered text message on your phone from your mum, aunt, friend, colleague asking if you've had that baby yet? Just refer them to: www.haveyouhadthatbabyyet.com.
- The due date they gave you at your first scan. Seriously, let it go in your mind and delete it from your calendar because you are not an oven timer.

Now go and have a bath or a nap.

BUMP PHOTO 6 → WEEK 40

Potentially this could be your very last bump photo! How crazy is that? This is a nice moment to reflect on all the photos you have taken and have hopefully printed out for this journal. Remind yourself how clever your body is and thank it for getting to this point – you are amazing!

How does your bump look to you now? Is it as big as you thought it would be? Do you think you're carrying quite high/low/round?

What have you found to be the most challenging part of your pregnancy, physically?

What has surprised you the most about your body?
Anything you've loved?

STICK YOUR
BUMP PHOTO
HERE

· · · · · · · · · · · · · ·

OK, so maybe you didn't think you'd still be pregnant by this stage. Maybe you thought naively that because you're super-organised and never late for a meeting or appointment that this baby would come a week early. Or that since your period is never late and you've always been regular like clockwork, your baby will be bang on time. Well, sadly, none of those theories are true and, on this occasion, it really is all down to your body, which you don't have much control over. This can be really annoying and frustrating, since there's only so many times you can unpack and re-pack the hospital bag and check the drawers full of white babygros are folded neatly...

Without a doubt, you will have heard from well-meaning friends and family that there are ways you can help to bring on labour, so here are the good, the bad and the ugly. Tick off the ones you've tried!

○ Eating pineapple, and I mean the whole pineapple, small chunks just won't do it.

○ The hottest curry you can eat, think five-starred chillies.

○ Drinking raspberry leaf tea (you'll never be able to drink it ever again).

○ Driving around in a car and going over speed bumps.

○ Walking for miles, up hills, ideally.

- Bouncing up and down on your birthing ball.
- Reflexology.
- Acupuncture.
- Clary sage oil – either in a massage, sniffed on a pillow or as drops in the bath.
- Eating dates.
- Holding other people's new-born babies and sniffing their heads like a maniac.
- A membrane sweep, or sometimes you need several, from your midwife.
- Walking up and down the stairs sideways.
- Nipple stimulation, either by hand, a pump or ask your partner to have a go?
- Sex: probably the last thing you want to do at this stage of pregnancy, but you'll try anything.
- Willpower. Have a serious chat to your bump: 'COME ON BABY, I'm done now.'

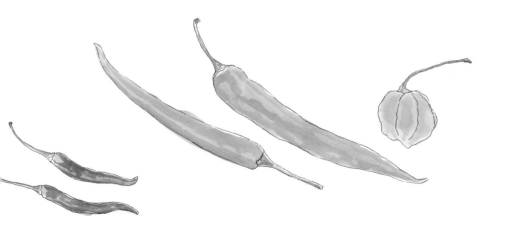

GOING OVERDUE

When it comes to having babies, all women would probably agree that 'going overdue' is the worst bit of all. Everyone wants to talk about it but also tells you to 'relax'. NOT HELPFUL AT ALL. It becomes THE talking point. Your postman, your neighbour, the lady in the supermarket, will all, without a doubt, ask you 'still pregnant then?' Um… let me just check my vagina…

Your midwife will also start to talk to you about your options when it comes to going 'post date', and the word 'induction' will be mentioned. Remember that even though being induced is a recommendation, it doesn't mean you have to do it. You have options, you have a voice and you can choose how this next week is managed so you feel empowered and supported.

TRUST THE PROCESS

Feeling anxious is the last thing you need, as cortisol and adrenaline (our stress hormones) can actually prevent you from going into labour. Focus on endorphins and oxytocin (the love hormone) to get you back in the zone. Connect with your baby, tell it that everything is going to be OK and that you can't wait to meet him or her. Disconnect from all those around you who are inhibiting you from feeling relaxed. Draw up the drawbridge, zone out and listen to your body. Thank your body for doing such an fantastic job and for working exactly as it should be: powerfully, comfortably and effectively. You're so close to holding your baby in your arms, so trust your body and baby to work together for this final stage. You're almost there. You've almost done it.

How are you feeling? Have you found this stage particularly tiring, emotional, exciting, scary?

Is there anything that has helped you relax? Is there anything that you find unhelpful?

What fun things have you done to distract yourself?

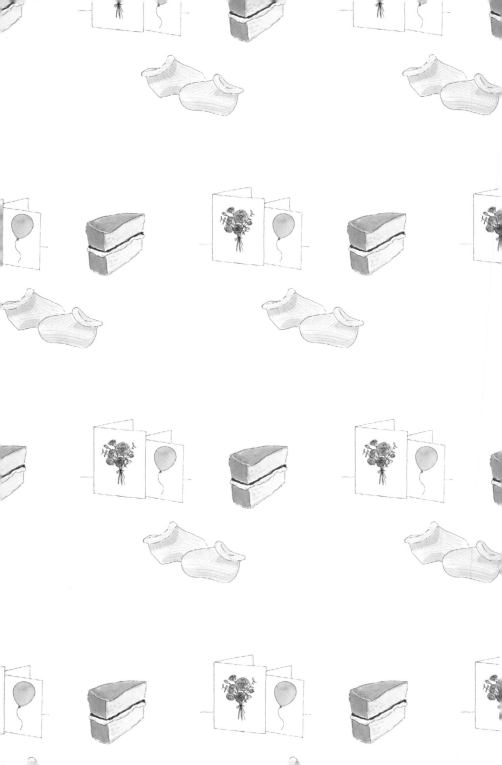

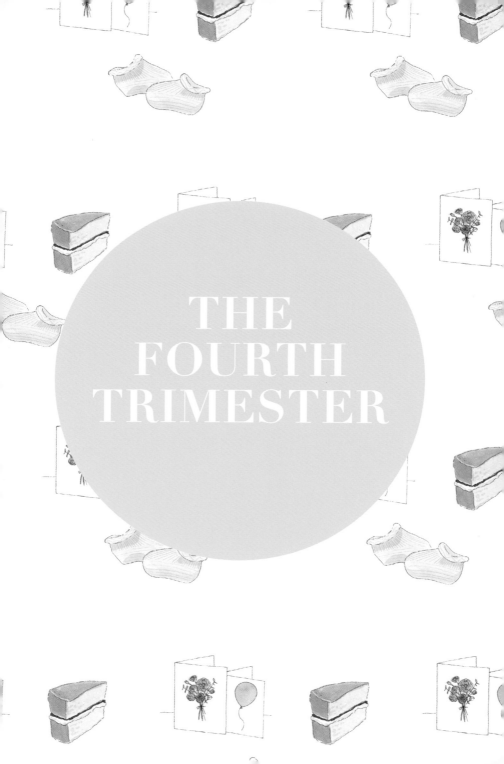

THE
FOURTH
TRIMESTER

COMING HOME

Nothing can quite prepare you for the surreal moment when you come home from hospital with that tiny brand-new person. It can almost feel like you've been given someone else's baby and that the hospital is going to call you any minute to tell you to return it. Or if you've had a home birth, you may be wondering when the midwife is going to take the baby away and you find yourself asking in disbelief whether you really just gave birth on the sofa/bedroom floor/in a pool in your living room?

But this is your baby. Welcome to the fourth trimester.

The fourth trimester starts from the moment your baby is born until he or she is three months old. Now you have a baby to care for every day, all those little but important milestones for both of you often get forgotten or missed, falling way down the list after the endless nappy changes and early-morning feeds. So, in this final part of the journal, there will be specific sections to fill in throughout so you can record all those milestones. You can go back and write them retrospectively but try to document as much as you can as you go along as they are such lovely moments to look back on and remember in years to come. Trust me, you forget so much!

I've also included space for you and your partner to write your baby's birth story. Wait until you are both ready, but try not to leave it too long after the event as it will be more difficult to remember all the details. Sharing the experience from both sides will bring a whole new perspective and you'll probably find that you remember very different things.

One thing I always remind new mums is that it is vital to treat the fourth trimester as a recovery period. Having a baby is a HUGE deal no matter how your birth went. Your body needs time to heal; your life has been turned upside down and this takes time to adjust to. Depending on your partner's situation, they may only get one or two weeks leave before going back to work, so use this time wisely. Below are my all-time top tips for when it comes to the early weeks. It took me more than ten years of being a midwife and having four of my own babies to realise these things make sense:

- 1 week in bed, 1 week on the sofa. There is no better time to enforce this rule than after you've had a baby. You have just gone through a major but amazing event and now you're caring not for just you but also for a tiny human who is relying on you 24/7. It's a massive deal. There will be PLENTY of time to take the baby out in the pram/sling/car to meet pals for a coffee but now is the time to rest and be with your new family.

- Visitors – choose them wisely. They can be a great asset at this time but, in reality, it's exhausting seeing people when you've been up all night, are still sore from the birth and learning how to achieve the perfect latch when breastfeeding. So keep it to the absolute VIP list, the rest can wait and, trust me, when your partner is back at work that is exactly when you want people popping in. If it's hard to manage your family's excitement, send them endless photos and videos via email or text. We are blessed with technology nowadays and this should keep them calm until you're ready to see people.

Be vocal and ask for help with feeding. When the midwife comes to see you at home, get them to watch you position and feed your baby. They are the experts and a tiny tweak in the position of the latch can make all the difference. Also remember all the support you looked into while you were pregnant (see page 104).

Accept that, at least initially, lots of babies don't like to sleep in their Moses basket or crib. They have lived inside you where it's warm, dark and comforting. They want to be close to you (or your partner), so instead of cursing the bloody Moses basket you bought, hold your baby, feed your baby in bed and get someone such as your community midwife or an experienced mum/aunt/ friend to show you how to swaddle your baby burrito-style!

Low maintenance EVERYTHING: house work (get a visitor to unload the dishwasher), cooking (open the freezer and enjoy!), appearance (PJs or comfy clothes for as long as possible) – and don't even bother with make-up in the early days. It really doesn't matter. What matters is that you're rested and not stressing about the less important things.

Sleep when the baby sleeps. I know this has been mentioned a lot before but it's the only way to cope with the broken nights. In the day, new-born babies often sleep a lot, so take these opportunities to get back into bed, cancel any visitors, turn your phone off and snooze.

COMING HOME QUESTIONS

How did you feel when you first came home from the hospital?

- -

- -

- -

Or if you had a home birth, how did you feel that very first night with your baby?

- -

- -

- -

What was your baby's first outfit?

- -

- -

What did you do on the first night?

Did you get any sleep?

How did you choose your baby's name? When did you decide?

Who were your first visitors?

Did anyone bring you any gifts?

BABY'S DETAILS

Full name

· · · · · · · · · · · · · · · · · · · ·

· · · · · · · · · · · · · · · · · · · ·

Date and time when
your baby was born

· · · · · · · · · · · · · · · · · · ·

· · · · · · · · · · · · · · · ·

Weight

· · · · · · · · · · · · · · · · · · ·

Length

· · · · · · · · · · · · · · · · · · ·

Head circumference

· · · · · · · · · · · · · · ·

Apgar score

· · · · · · · · · · · · · · · · · · ·

Vitamin K injection
or oral drops?

. . . .

Time of first feed
and for how long?

. . . .

. . . .

First meconium poo
and wee?

. . . .

Birth stone

. . . .

Meaning of name

. . . .

Star sign

. . . .

FIRST BABY PHOTOS

WRITING YOUR BIRTH STORY

Try not to leave it too long before writing your birth story as it's amazing how quickly you can forget the details. To help you, here are some useful prompt questions. On the next few pages is space for you and your partner to write your experience of what happened.

QUESTIONS FOR YOU:

- When and how did you go into labour? Did your waters break? Contractions? A show?
- When and how did you know when to call the midwife?
- How did your contractions feel?
- What positions or self-help methods did you find helpful? Perhaps some massage, TENS or hypnobirthing?
- And what didn't help at all?
- Who were your midwives?
- Did you use your birth preferences to guide you?
- Was there any music playing when your baby was born?
- Can you remember anything else distinctive? The colour of the room? A picture on the wall?

- How did you feel as soon as you met your baby?
- What did she/he look like and smell like?
- What did your partner do during labour and delivery?

QUESTIONS FOR YOUR PARTNER:

- Where were you when your partner told you she was in labour?
- How did you feel? Excited, nervous, scared, READY?
- Did anything you've read in the books or online help you feel prepared?
- How did you support your partner during labour?
- What did it feel like when you saw your baby for the first time?
- Did you cut the cord?
- Did you have skin-to-skin?
- What did your baby look like?

YOUR BIRTH STORY

YOUR PARTNER'S
BIRTH STORY

THE 2/3/4 AM FEED

There's a secret night club you're invited to! It's so exclusive that no one talks about it when you're pregnant but now you're a mama, your name is at the top of the guest list. Welcome to the night-time feeding club.

Whether you're breast- or bottle-feeding, without a doubt you'll be up winding, changing or soothing your newborn baby during those magical early hours. It can sometimes feel a bit lonely, especially if your partner is snoring through the commotion of a double nappy change and feeding marathon. Not to mention EXHAUSTING. But know that you are far from alone!

It's very normal for babies to want to feed a lot during the night and I don't know many babies who feed every three hours on the hour – mine certainly didn't. Some feeds seem to roll straight into the next so try to doze as much as you can in-between to help combat that tiredness. Many women often reach for their phone to help them stay awake during night feeds – the blue light emitted from your screen makes your brain ping alive and think it's waking-up time. However, this can make it harder to go back to sleep after you've settled your baby and the last thing you want is a peacefully sleeping baby while you've been sucked down a social media rabbit hole and are still wide awake...

SOME TIPS TO KEEP THINGS QUIET DURING A NIGHT FEED INCLUDE:

- Only use low-level lighting, such a night light or LED candles – anything that won't over-stimulate you or your baby.

- Download an app that turns off the blue light on your phone after 11pm.

- Drop some lavender oil on your pillow to help bring on sleep when you've settled your baby after feeding.

- If you're bottle-feeding, share the load with your partner some nights – maybe at the weekends when they don't have to get up for work the next day.

Sometimes, though, those night feeds can be a bit tough, and you might find yourself needing some light entertainment or distraction to keep you going. I once did an entire online food shop and forgot what I ordered until the next day when 36 loo rolls, a dragon fruit and 4 kilos of penne pasta arrived at my front door. So, be warned: online shopping when you're tired can cause you to order obscure things!

SOME IDEAS I FOUND REALLY HELPFUL WHEN I WAS UP FEEDING INCLUDE:

- Listening to some brilliant podcasts, the funnier the better.

- Playing your labour playlist or creating a new playlist with some relaxing music (this also helps you to stay calm and feel sleepy).

- Listening to your hypnobirthing relaxation tracks.

- Reading a light and easy book.

- Messaging your mum/pals to see who else is up. I found it really helpful and reassuring connecting to other mums going through the same challenges as me – and they were a constant source of top tips, advice and inspiration. It was great not to feel alone!

How are you feeling?

_____

_____

How is the feeding going?

_____

_____

_____

What help have you had?

_____

How much is your baby sleeping and how much are you sleeping?

_____

_____

How does your postpartum body look and feel?

_____

_____

Is it how you expected to look/feel one week postpartum?

_____

_____

How are you recovering physically?

_____

_____

What has surprised you the most about having a newborn baby?

_____

_____

_____

How do you feel you've bonded with your baby?

_____

_____

_____

What have you done with your baby so far?

_____

What have been the highs and lows of this first week?

_____

_____

_____

_____

THIS WEEK REMEMBER TO:

- Register the birth.
- Register the baby at the doctor's.
- Book your 6-week postnatal appointment with your GP.
- Start doing your pelvic-floor exercises (doing them while you feed is a good idea!).

BABY BLUES

I'm sure you've heard of the expression 'baby blues'. It generally means when you feel a bit weepy, usually around the time your milk comes in (around day five) and your hormones go mental. But sometimes it doesn't happen at that time and without any warning, two weeks later the tears come flooding and you just don't know why.

Post-baby hormones do crazy things to our minds. Some women never get weepy and ride on a tidal wave of oxytocin for weeks and feel on cloud nine – but then the broken sleep end relentless feeding-winding-changing-repeat routine starts to feel a little like Ground Hog Day. And you might feel a bit miffed at your partner going back to work, and suddenly the thought of being at home on the sofa all day and not showering and getting dressed until past midday fills you with dread.

What is important to understand is that it is OK not to feel amazing every day because that's not the reality of having a baby. You might feel great in the morning and want visitors or even venture out to the local café for coffee and cake. But by the time you get home, you're sore, and you've leaked through onto your top because you've forgotten to wear breast pads and the last thing you want is your husband's brother and his girlfriend coming over.

So really listen to your hormones and your body and think about what's important right now. Going back to bed is often a great idea.

Turn off your phone for a bit or at least hand over any admin to your partner, such as replying to messages and calls. People aren't going to expect you to be back on form two weeks after you've had a baby. Be honest: cancel visitors and say 'I'm just so tired I'm going to have a sleep' or 'we want to have a day for just us today'. Try listening to your hypnobirthing relaxation tracks, as it will get you back into that chilled space you were in when you were pregnant.

Maybe you're questioning whether or not to swaddle your baby, or does your baby even like swaddling or are you feeding your baby frequently enough or is your baby pooing enough or is that wind/colic/reflux? All mums, whether it's their first or fourth baby, will go

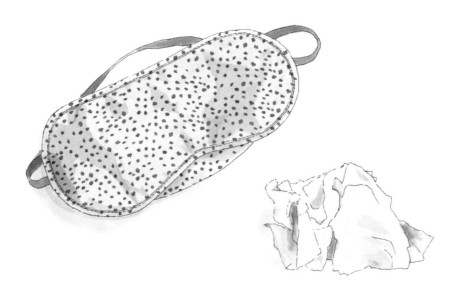

through the motions, questioning and doubting pretty much everything they do. Motherhood will always pose these challenges and you'll work through them. You are doing bloody brilliantly.

And if these baby blues aren't lasting just a few days and you're feeling like a thick black cloud of worry, anxiety and doubt are hanging over you, TALK TO SOMEONE. Anyone you feel you can open up to: a close friend, your mum, your sister, your partner, a health professional. Don't wait for your midwife to visit and ask you if you're OK; call them and ask for help. Becoming a mum is a massive deal. It's a happy time but it can feel overwhelming and if that feeling doesn't go away and you find yourself not feeling how you thought you'd feel, don't be ashamed. No one is going to judge you or tell you you're probably just tired (and if they do, speak to someone else, a different GP or midwife).

LACTATION COOKIES

. . . .

These contain three ingredients many people believe encourage milk production – flaxseeds, oats and brewer's yeast. Definitely worth a try and they taste delicious too! The oats are also great for slow-release energy to see you through those long nights…

Makes 10
75g oats | 45g self-raising flour | 2 tbsp ground flaxseeds
40g brown sugar | 2 tbsp brewer's yeast
1 tsp ground cinnamon | 1 medium egg | 2 tbsp maple syrup
30g chocolate chips

Preheat the oven to 160°C(fan)/180°C/gas mark 4. Line a baking tray with baking paper.

Combine the oats, flour, flaxseeds, sugar, brewer's yeast and cinnamon in a bowl. In a separate small bowl, whisk together the egg and maple syrup. Pour the wet mixture into the dry, along with the chocolate chips and combine to make a sticky dough.

Spoon little mounds onto your lined baking tray, leaving space between them as they will spread in the oven. Press them down slightly with the back of your spoon. Cook in the oven for 10–15 minutes until lightly browned. Leave to cool on the tray for 5 minutes, then cool completely on a wire rack and keep in an airtight container for up to a week.

AVOCADO, BANANA, OATS AND BERRIES SMOOTHIE

• • • • • • • • • • • • • •

This is a super-quick meal in a glass for when you don't have time
for a proper breakfast. Use whatever berries you like and add a
little honey or maple syrup if you're craving something sweet.
It is packed with healthy fats, protein, calcium, slow-release
energy, fibre, potassium, manganese and vitamins B6, C and E.

Serves 1
1 small banana, sliced then frozen | ½ avocado
1 small handful fresh or frozen berries | 2 tbsp porridge oats
2 tsp chia seeds (optional) | 250ml milk of your choice

Blend together until thick and creamy.

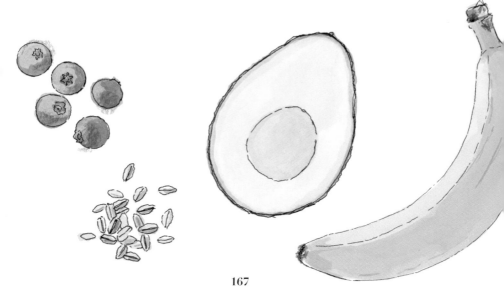

THE SECOND WEEK

How have you felt in the second week?

Is there anything you've struggled with?

What have been your high points?

And any low points?

What did you need the most? Sleep? Chocolate biscuits?

How are you recovering physically?

Did you have any visitors?

What have you done with your baby?

What is your favourite thing about your baby?

How has your relationship with your partner evolved?

I am exactly what
my child needs.

Each day I learn and grow as a mother.

THE THIRD WEEK

How are you feeling in the third week?

What were the high points?

And any low points?

How are you recovering?

Is there anything you feel has become easier or more enjoyable this week?

Have you been on an outing yet?

What do you like doing with your baby?

What is your favourite outfit for your baby?

1 MONTH OLD

A month. Four weeks. Thirty-odd days. You've been going at this motherhood thing for a while now and just look how far you've come. Never underestimate how brilliant you are, right now. Just take a moment and say out loud 'I am amazing'.

This past month may have been harder and more challenging than you imagined. How can something approximately 50cm long and weighing around eight pounds change your life so much that even the simplest of tasks, such a making a cup of tea and actually remembering to drink it hot, have become so tricky.

Nothing can prepare you for quite how much your life changes when you become a mother; the way you feel and react to things, the shift in your routine, the way you view your body, the unconditional love you have towards something so tiny that depends on you 100 per cent, the exhaustion. Yet you keep on going, muddling through, trying out different techniques and options until you *think* you've got the hang of it all. But, remember, you'll never get it right all of the time, and that's OK – in fact, that's normal. We're only human after all.

So try and have a flexible approach to mothering. You may want to start venturing out a bit more around now, meeting up with some mum mates you've met, trying some local breastfeeding support

groups, going to the baby clinic – anything that gets you out of the house for a few hours a day. Sometimes all you need is a bit of adult conversation and someone else to make you a cup of tea. And on the days when you can't get out of the house and your baby seems to want to feed on the hour every hour, don't push yourself. Stay indoors, hunker down and enjoy these days. Everyone will tell you this, but it really does go so quickly and before you know it, your tiny baby will be crawling and walking and need entertaining at baby singing groups so enjoy this special time together.

What have you and your baby achieved – however small –
this past week?

Who have you seen?

Any major breakthroughs?

Anything that's got easier over the past month?

How is your body healing?

How is your relationship with your partner developing?

_____

_____

What were the high and low points of the past month?

_____

_____

What are you going to miss from the newborn phase?

_____

_____

What is your baby like? Is there anything he or she loves to do?

_____

_____

Any favourite new-mum hangouts?

_____

_____

BABY PHOTOS 1 MONTH

MILESTONES FOR MUM

○ Showered and dressed (in normal clothes not PJs) before noon.

○ Remembered to wear breast pads.

○ Learnt how to fold and unfold the pram.

○ Remembered your baby's red book for the health visitor clinic.

○ Went to the supermarket and did the weekly shop with your baby staying asleep the entire time.

○ Successfully fed your baby in public without feeling self-conscious.

○ Wrote some thank you cards for your baby presents and actually posted them.

○ Opened a conversation with your new mum mates with 'what colour is your baby's poo?'

○ Prepared lunch for yourself and ate it one-handed while holding your baby.

○ Finished your all-time favourite six-series box set (and then wonderied what to watch next!).

Can you believe it?! Can you even remember what your life was like pre-baby? How do you feel when you look back and think of yourself holding your newborn in your arms for the first time? Does it feel like yesterday or does it feel much longer ago than just two months? Although while you are experiencing it, day-to-day life when you are looking after a new baby can sometimes feel like it's passing quite slowly, I bet you're a little bit surprised to realise that your baby is two months old already!

If you haven't had it yet, you will be coming up to your 6–8 week GP check-up. This appointment is for you to discuss how the birth went, how your body is healing, how feeding is going and your general mood. Your GP will also give your baby a head-to-toe check over. Use this opportunity to ask any questions you have. Some things to consider asking at this appointment include:

- Any issues or concerns with your vagina and perineum – how are your healing down there? They can check any stiches have healed well too.
- Pelvic-floor exercises – are you doing them properly?
- If you had a C-section, ask your GP to check your scar.
- Contraception! I know it sounds early, but it's really important you've thought about your options so you don't get caught out in the heat of the moment...

In what ways are you feeling more confident as a mum?

What do you like to do with your baby? Where do you like to go?

How does your partner like to get involved?

What have been the highs and lows this month?

How has your baby changed over the past month?

BABY PHOTOS 2 MONTHS

3 MONTHS: YOU'VE DONE IT!

You've reached the end of the fourth trimester! Achieving this massive milestone in your journey into motherhood is definitely worth a huge pat on the back (or glass of wine/gin/bar of chocolate/day off from changing a nappy).

No doubt there have been plenty of tears (from both you and your baby) and plenty of moments of 'am I doing this right?' and 'I'm not sure I'm good enough'. Motherhood will and does constantly present you with challenges, surprise you and leave you feeling a little bit dazed at times – but you'll always find a way to work through it! Remember, you are doing the hardest job in the world but you're not alone. Find your mum mates – your girl gang who will inspire you, lift you up on the days when you're doubting yourself, celebrate the achievements large and small, and always reply to your 'Anyone else up feeding?' messages at 3am.

Just look how far you've come. You're doing brilliantly so you should be really proud of yourself.

What are you most proud of so far?

How are you ensuring you remember to look after yourself?

How have you spent some baby-free time?

Who are your girl gang/mum mates?

Have you joined any baby classes?

What's the best thing about being on maternity leave?

How is your partner bonding with the baby?

How has your relationship with your partner developed
over the past 3 months?

Have you had a date night (without the baby)?

What has been the hardest challenge of being a new mum?

And what have been your favourite parts?

_____

_____

Any surprising things about being a mum?

_____

_____

What does your baby love to do?

_____

_____

Do you think he or she looks like either you or your partner?

_____

_____

What are you most looking forward to in the next 3/6/9 months?

_____

_____

BABY'S FIRSTS

First bath

First sounds

First outing

First smile

First laugh

First slept through the night

First rolled over

First tooth

First sat up

First crawl

First solid food

First stood up

First words

First walked

First shoes

First holiday

First Christmas

First birthday activity

Weight record

At birth		7 months	
1 month		8 months	
2 months		9 months	
3 months		10 months	
4 months		11 months	
5 months		1 year	
6 months			

Clemmie is a midwife at King's College Hospital. She writes the successful blog www.gasandairblog.com and lives with her four daughters and husband in Kent. Her first book was *How to Grow a Baby and Push It Out*.

 @mother_of_daughters

10 9 8 7 6 5 4 3 2 1

Vermilion, an imprint of Ebury Publishing, 20 Vauxhall Bridge Road, London SW1V 2SA

Vermilion is part of the Penguin Random House group of companies whose addresses can be found at global. penguinrandomhouse.com

Penguin
Random House
UK

Text © Clemmie Hooper, 2018

First published in the United Kingdom by Vermilion in 2018

A CIP catalogue record for this book is available from the British Library

www.penguin.co.uk

Commissioning editor: Sam Jackson
Project editor: Laura Herring / Book design by Myfanwy Vernon-Hunt / Illustrations by Zoe Barker / yesmum® affirmation cards on pages 92–93 and 170–171 by Hollie de Cruz

ISBN 9781785041617

Colour reproduction by Altaimage Ltd. Printed and bound in China by Toppan Leefung

Penguin Random House is committed to a sustainable future for our business, our readers and our planet. This book is made from Forest Stewardship Council® certified paper.

MIX
Paper from
responsible sources
FSC® C018179
www.fsc.org